RV LIVING

MASTER THE LIFE ON THE ROAD

WRITTEN BY

Mitch Sargood

The follow book is reproduced below with the goal of providing information that is as accurate and reliable as possible. Regardless, purchasing this book can be seen as consent to the fact that both the publisher and the author of this book are in no way experts on the topics discussed within and that any recommendations or suggestions that are made herein are for entertainment purposes only. Professionals should be consulted as needed prior to undertaking any of the action endorsed herein.

This declaration is deemed fair and valid by both the American Bar Association and the Committee of Publishers Association and is legally binding throughout the United States.

Furthermore, the transmission, duplication or reproduction of any of the following work including specific information will be considered an illegal act irrespective of if it is done electronically or in print. This extends to creating a secondary or tertiary copy of the work or a recorded copy and is only allowed with express written consent from the Publisher. All additional right reserved.

The information in the following pages is broadly considered to be a truthful and accurate account of facts and as such any inattention, use or misuse of the information in question by the reader will render any resulting actions solely under their purview. There are no scenarios in which the publisher or the original author of this work can be in any fashion deemed liable for any hardship or damages that may befall them after undertaking information described herein.

Additionally, the information in the following pages is intended only for informational purposes and should thus be thought of as universal. As befitting its nature, it is presented without assurance regarding its prolonged validity or interim quality. Trademarks that are mentioned are done without written consent and can in no way be considered an endorsement from the trademark holder.

TABLE OF CONTENTS

INTRODUCTION

C ongratulations on purchasing this book and thank you for doing so.

The following chapters will discuss everything you need to know about what life is like on the road living in an RV full time. If you are thinking about buying your very first RV to hit the road in, then you're going to find this book a useful guide to help you get started.

Living a life on the road can be an adventure full of wonderful and exciting new experiences as you roll through the country in your mobile motorhome. But owning an RV isn't as simple as just renting or purchasing your vehicle, turning the keys and hitting the road. There are a lot more responsibility and considerations that come with owning an RV that you may not even be aware of.

In this book, we will take a look at the types of RVs on the market and how to choose your first one, what the legal considerations of living in an RV are, and the pros and cons of RV life so you'll be able to see if this is, in fact, the life for you. This book also includes with it a first-time RV owner's checklist of what to look out for, meal prep tips and ideas for the road and more.

There are plenty of books on this subject on the market, thanks again for choosing this one! Every effort was made to ensure it is full of as much useful information as possible, please enjoy!

CHAPTER ONE

YOUR FIRST RV - CHOOSING ONE THAT'S PERFECT FOR YOU

S o, you've decided to ditch the conventional home living and adopt the nomadic lifestyle of being on the road and living in an RV. Great! Now comes one of the most difficult aspects of your journey – what kind of RV should you choose?

If you've already started shopping around for your new RV, you probably would have already realized by now that it isn't going to be as simple as picking out one that looks good and plonking down the money for it. Choosing your first RV is much like choosing your first home. Sure, it may not technically be the same thing, but the concept is similar. Just like a home, you would need to assess your current lifestyle, budget, and needs, determine what you're looking for and from there narrow down your selection to one that is going to meet all your criteria.

The first few questions that you would need to ask are:

- What type of RV should you go for? The big rig or the camper van version?
- Should you be driving the Class A version, the B Class or the Class C option? Or would a bus conversion or travel trailer be better suited to what you have in mind?

FACTORS TO CONSIDER BEFORE BUYING YOUR FIRST RV

Selecting the right RV and weighing the options could take hours, days or months of research on online forums, articles and even consumer reports and reviews. To make things much easier on the first-time RV owner, the list of questions below will help you answer some questions you may not even have considered when deciding to buy your first RV.

WHAT CAMPING STYLE ARE YOU CONSIDERING?

The first thing you would need to do is decide whether you are going to be living in an RV full-time or whether it is just a temporary vacation situation. The option you choose will be the deciding factor about which type of RV you should get. If you're going with the full-time RV living option, you would choose to get something bigger to be able to carry what you need because this is going to be your mobile home for the foreseeable future, as opposed to if the RV was just for a short-term vacation and you would bring only what you need with you on the trip and nothing more.

HOW MUCH TRAVELING DO YOU PLAN TO DO?

Do you plan to be active on the move, never staying at one place for more than a week or two? Or would you prefer to settle in a location for some time before heading out on the road again? In this instance, remember that using a bigger RV and traveling more often would cost you more fuel. If you are planning to live in an RV full time, but settle in one location for a long period until you feel the need to move elsewhere, you are going to want an RV that will be able to meet your everyday living needs. Opt for an RV that comes with large holding tanks that are built sturdy if this is going to be your full-time residence. If an RV is just for a short-term period or vacation, perhaps, a smaller version that is better built for camping and being on the move all the time would be a more suitable choice.

WHERE ARE YOU PLANNING TO LIVE?

When living in an RV, it is important to plan ahead where your stops are going to be and where you would prefer to camp out as soon as you reach your destination. It isn't as simple as just driving to the nearest parking spot and stopping there for the night. Some states have prepared designated areas where RVs can spend their time at. If you were planning to stay at public parks for RVs for the majority of your journey, you might want to consider an RV that is about 32 feet and below since the public spaces are usually not able to accommodate anything bigger than that. Campers, camper vans, and small travel trailers are going to be your best choice for public park parking since smaller RVs make it easy to park just about anywhere without worrying that you may be bothering other RV travelers by taking up more space than you should. The larger classes of RV like the Class A, for example, work much better in a full-amenity RV park setting or even just the outdoors if there is a space that's big enough to allow you to settle your RV in for a couple of days.

ARE YOU TRAVELING SOLO OR WITH COMPANY?

Traveling solo and bringing others with you are going to have an impact on the choice of RV you select. If you are traveling with a partner, with kids or even with pets, you are going to need a bigger RV that is going to accommodate these needs, especially where children and pets are concerned. If you are traveling with two or more people in your company, you may want to consider the bunkhouse style, Class A or Class C RV options.

WHERE WOULD BE THE BEST PLACE TO BUY AN RV?

Your best bet would be to frequent RV shows and dealers to see what's available. RV shows are great especially when you're doing your research into buying your first RV. The shows usually take place in the spring, summer or fall all over the country and it is a great way to take note of the different styles, builds and choices in one convenient location. You should definitely consider frequenting a couple of shows before attempting to purchase your first RV as it will give you a much better perspective. There are also plenty of RV dealers around that will have a variety of RVs at their dealership for you to take a look at. They will not have all the models of course, but there will be a good variety on hand at least, so it is still a useful trip. Plus, you get to ask the salespeople all the questions you may have about each model, maybe even score some advice and tips since the salesperson would be the most knowledgeable source you have on hand. After all, they need to know what they're selling so they would be familiar with the vehicles inside and out.

SHOULD I BUY RIGHT AWAY?

For first time RV buyers, it is highly recommended that you test the waters by renting an RV first before you put down the money for one of your own. The last thing you want is to buy your first RV only to find out after a while that it actually isn't what you were looking for at all. Also, keep in mind that driving an RV isn't going to be like anything you're used to, especially if you have never driven anything bigger than a four-wheel drive before. Find a dealer that has a couple of models on hand that you could rent. This is a good way to get the feel of different models, and it'll give you a better understanding of what you're looking for as you narrow down your list.

ARE MY FINANCES READY FOR RV LIVING?

Before you set out buying your first RV, sit down, and take a good long look at your current financial state. Make a list of what expenses you can expect while you live in an RV and as you travel on the road. Are you going to be financing your RV purchase on your own? If not, you may want to determine your budget beforehand and how much you're willing to set aside each month for the loan payment of the RV. That would help you narrow down your choices to select an RV that is able to suit your lifestyle and your budget at the same time.

OTHER FACTORS TO CONSIDER WHEN LIVING IN AN RV

Living in an RV is more than just purchasing one, taking the keys, packing your stuff and you're good to go. You will soon quickly find out that there is quite a lot more to consider and it isn't just as simple as driving and deciding where you're going to spend the next couple of days.

Here's a list of what else you need to keep in mind about life in an RV:

- **Miles & Fuel** – The bigger the RV, the more you are going to expect to spend on fuel. If fuel is one of your concerns, consider an RV that is going to be the most economical for your budget where you will be able to get the most miles per gallon.

- **Maintenance** – Again, the bigger the RV, the more you can expect to fork out on maintenance and upkeep. Be prepared for maintenance to be costly at times, unless you're ready to be your own handyman.

- **Insurance** – The bigger the RV, the more your insurance fees are going to be. Shop around at several insurance companies and find the best rate for you.

- **Price Range** – Just like buying a car, you could easily fall in love with all the features that the RV has to offer. Until you see the price. The better the RV, the most costly it is going to be.

- **Camping Costs** – Not all places that you'll be camped out at are going to be free. Set aside a budget for camping and research beforehand how much it is going to cost you to park at certain locations. In some instances, the cost would depend on the size of your RV. The bigger the RV, the more expensive it will be.

- **Towing Costs** – Sometimes these things happen, and there may be moments where your RV needs to be towed. Or there may be instances where you could end up towing another RV behind yours. Whatever the situation may be, be prepared financially and with the right equipment on hand, so you're ready for any emergency.

- **Parking Issues** – Bigger RVs are harder to park and harder to fit into spaces. Again, it's helpful in this instance to check out the location of your next destination ahead of time, so you don't arrive and get stuck because you have no place to park. If you are thinking about getting an RV for vacation purposes, you would need to park it at home before you head out on your journey. A lot of homeowner associations do not accommodate RVs in the area so if yours doesn't, rent a storage facility ahead of time where you can park your RV until you need it.

- **Cooking** – Remember that an RV is a smaller version of a home, which means it's going to come with a smaller – much smaller – kitchen area. You won't be able to cook the fancy meals you may have done at home, but you will still be able to prepare decent meals and even have fun cooking outdoors sometimes.

- **Lack of Connectivity** – Be prepared to part with consistently good internet and Wi-Fi connection. That is one luxury you may not be able to get all the time while you're on the road. If it is within your budget, you can decide to have your RV fitted with mobile internet or Wi-Fi boosters, but the connection may not be as great or as stable as the one you would get at home.

CHOICES OF RVS AVAILABLE

Once you've settled on the idea of buying an RV and you've made a list of all the things you should be aware of, there's still the matter of selecting the right RV. Here are some of the RVs that are available on the market:

CLASS A MOTORHOMES

These models have just about every amenity you need and are the ideal option for long distance traveling with a family. Class A motorhomes are usually fitted with captain's chairs, a full-sized fridge, oven, microwave, stove, large sofa, dining table, television, kitchen countertops, bathrooms with toilet flushes, queen sized beds, closet space and more. You get what you pay for though, so be prepared to spend an upwards of $60,000 for these babies.

CLASS B MOTORHOMES

This model offers many similar features to their Class A counterparts, but in a smaller, more manageable package. Similar to driving a large SUV, the Class B option is best suited for two or three travelers at a time.

CLASS C MOTORHOMES

This model is a cross or a combination of the Class A and Class B variants and is one of the more popular options to rent during the summer. It is easy enough to maneuver with just enough room for the family to sleep. The 40-foot version of these motorhomes can rival what you get with the Class A models, only with a much cheaper price tag.

TRAVEL, FIFTH-WHEEL & POP-UP TRAILERS

Travel trailers have the advantage of being lightweight, yet sturdy and they are one of the more towable options. They can easily be towed by the standard pickup trucks, SUVs or even minivans. These models are able to hold up to six sleepers.

Fifth-wheel trailers are named as such because of the hitch pin that can be attached to the trailer via a special mount. It is also a much easier model to back into a campsite compared to the conventional trailer. Fifth-wheelers can be anywhere from 18 to 40 feet long.

Pop-up trailers are the smallest and lightest of all the trailer options and are one of the most economical models to own. The price of these trailers can start as low as $4,000, and the smallest version of these variants are easily towable with a minivan. Thanks to its size, it is also one of the easier models to park.

TRUCK CAMPERS

When it comes to mobile traveling, it doesn't get any better than truck campers. These campers can go where motorhomes and trailers will not, while still being able to offer the basic comforts of a home at a fraction of what it would cost you to purchase a motorhome.

SURV TRAILER

The trailer version of an SUV, the SURV is short for Sports Utility RV that comes with a garage built into the rear of the trailer. The garage is a useful space and comes in handy when storing motorcycles, bicycles, quad bikes and more for the adventure seeker who plans on doing a lot of outdoor activities while on the road.

CHAPTER TWO

RV VS. HOUSES – WHICH IS THE BETTER CHOICE?

At first, not everyone may be taken with the idea of living in an RV instead of the good old standard American home. After all, hasn't the perfect scenario we've all had in our heads growing up consisted of graduating, getting a good job and buying our first home before starting a family of our own?

Why would an RV possibly be better than living in a house? Because being rooted in just one location for the rest of your life may not be everyone's ideal scenario. In fact, there are people who prefer the freedom of being able to be on the move whenever they like. Which would explain why RV living would be a very appealing option to them.

REASONS WHY LIVING IN AN RV IS BETTER THAN A HOUSE

RV life on the road can be an adventure. It makes you feel like the world is yours for the taking. You can go anywhere you want, anytime and have the added bonus of bringing your home (well, sort of) with you on the road!

A Different View Every Morning – Imagine waking up in the mornings, and looking out your window to a different view each time you settle in a new location. That's what you would get when you live in an RV. One day, your view could be of breathtaking mountainsides, and another it could be of crystal blue waters as you look out at the vast ocean in front of you. Waking up to a different view every morning can leave you with a great feeling and a sense of freedom that money just can't buy. Plus, you feel like you're traveling but saving a bundle on having to pay for hotels or motels because hey, you've brought your mobile home with you!

You Appreciate the Little Things – When you're on the road, it's the little things like constant good Wi-Fi connection and a nice bathroom to shower in that you might miss the most. And missing these little life luxuries that a lot of people tend to take for granted because it has become so much a part of our everyday lives that we just don't notice them, makes you much more appreciative and grateful when you get to experience it again. It's good to be reminded once in a while to stop and take a moment to be grateful for the blessed life that we have been given.

No Mortgage – Paying off home loans and mortgages can be soul crushing. Especially when you're not making a bucket load of money. Those who live in an RV full time will tell you what a huge relief it is not to be tied down by the chains of having debt to pay off, especially when an RV – compared to the price of a home – is vastly cheaper, especially with the current housing market of today where home prices can be through the roof. Not having to pay off a huge mortgage also leaves you with more money left over to add to your retirement savings. Added bonus!

No Rent – This goes hand-in-hand with the point above about not having any mortgage to pay. If you think home loan prices are a killer, rent is not going to be any better. The price of rent has gotten so high, even in places like San Francisco, people have become forced to share cramped and tiny spaces just to save some money. And even then, rent is not any cheaper, just maybe slightly more affordable compared to renting your own apartment.

Fulfill Your American Bucket List – How many people have made it to all the states in America? America is a huge country, and you can bet that not everyone has had the opportunity to say that yes, they have set foot and spent some time in each and every single state that this beautiful country has to offer. Unless they live in an RV of course. When you can bring your home with you on the road, there is no reason not to visit the whole of America and cross that off your bucket list as an accomplishment that not everyone has had the privilege to experience. And there is no better way to experience all the best things that the country has to offer than when you're traveling on the road. Flying just doesn't cut it.

You Find Yourself Being Outdoors a Lot More – Let's face it, we're not exactly living the healthiest lifestyle in today's world. We lack sleep, are working long hours sitting behind our desks and gaining weight from all that unhealthy takeaway and fast food we have to consume because of our hectic lifestyle. And when we do get home at the end of the day, where do we end up? On the sofa in front of the TV, sitting again, for long hours binging on Netflix. Or at least, that's the average scenario if you were to live in a home. While living in an RV, there is no space to lounge about on your sofa being a couch potato because of the confined and limited space. Especially if you aren't traveling alone. That forces you (in a good way) to get out of your RV and take in the fresh air of the outdoors. For entertainment, you would go hiking, go for a swim, or even just go for long walks if the weather is particularly great on that day. Being outdoors, moving about doing some kind of activity is a much healthier lifestyle than living a sedentary life, and you would be feeling a lot fitter, better and healthier without you even realizing it.

Everyday Can Be an Adventure – The great thing about being on the move in your RV is looking forward to your next destination and anticipating what lies in store. Every day becomes a possible new adventure that is just waiting to happen. Living in an RV gives you freedom as you would never imagine, and such experiences are priceless.

You're Cleaner – Having dirty dishes lying around the RV is a big NO. Because of the smaller space, leaving unwashed dishes or even laundry is going to stink up the place pretty fast. This, in turn, will force you to clean up after using them almost immediately before things start to pile up and before you know it, becoming a neat freak will soon be a daily habit and a good one to have. No more leaving messes around like what tends to happen in a lot of homes!

Cleaning Becomes a Breeze – Anyone who detests cleaning and doing household chores will be dancing around in glee to find how much easier it is to clean an RV. Cleaning a house? It could take 2-3 hours, perhaps more depending on how big your home may be. Cleaning an RV? Give yourself a pat on the back because you could be done in 30 minutes or less.

You Save Big Money When It Comes to the Holiday Seasons – Having a home to decorate during the festive holidays is going to cost you a lot more than decorating an RV during those same holidays. Homes are bigger, and bigger means a larger space that you would need to fill up with décor. Although decorations may not be something we give a lot of thought to generally, if you add up your bills, you just might be surprised at how much you end up spending during the holidays. Yikes! Now compare that to your little RV, smaller space, smaller decorative bill. And all that extra money? Yup, you guessed it. Right into your savings account. Score!

You Become a Storyteller – Suddenly, you find that you've become much more interesting at parties and gatherings when everyone crowds around you eager to hear the stories and experiences you've had while living on the road in your RV. The places you've been, the things you've seen, the people you've met, what you've experienced both good and bad while being mobile are all great conversation starters. Plus, they're memories to last a lifetime. Experiences like that just don't come with owning a home.

It Teaches You to Live on Only the Essentials – Let's face it, an RV doesn't come with a lot of space. Which means you are only able to afford to have what you need to survive and there is just no room for clutter or space to store unnecessary things the way there would be in a home. Having to live on only the necessities and essentials can be a real eye-opener, and it shows just how much we have in our lives that we don't actually need and could have saved money on.

It Helps You Grow as A Person – Living in an RV means you always have to be prepared for the unexpected. While living in an RV has a lot of perks, there are going to be moments where things need to be fixed. Sometimes there may not always be a handyman or mechanic nearby when something goes wrong, and you are going to have to roll up your sleeves and get down and dirty learning how to repair things like radiators or generators, learn how to check your gauges, and a lot of other things that you may not otherwise have taken the trouble to learn if you were living comfortably in a home. Tough experiences are learning experiences, and it gives you a chance to see what you're made of and how you handle situations when the going gets tough. At the end of the day, it leaves you a much better person than you were when you started.

You Learn the True Value of Things – There's nothing like being on the road, living on the bare minimum and having to adapt to situations, places, and people as you go along to make you value just how important these aspects of your life are. Living on the road helps you realize that there are some experiences that money just can't buy. It teaches you how much you actually love your family and friends when you don't see them or talk to them as often as you would like, so when you do meet, you value the experience of being together so much more. It teaches you how not to waste money on unnecessary things, and what is important to survive on.

CHAPTER THREE

THE ULTIMATE RV CHECKLIST

R eady to get started with your first RV? Before you do, there is one thing that every first timer would need on hand – a good checklist. Or several checklists, if you really want to do a thorough job with your research.

There are a lot more considerations when buying an RV than you may think because you aren't just buying an RV, you're buying a vehicle and a home combined into one. Therefore, you can expect your checklist to be twice as long as it would have been if you were buying just a home or a new car.

BEFORE BUYING AN RV CHECKLIST

Here's a list of things you would need on your checklist to help you get started:

- **Define your goals** – Are you planning to live in your RV full time, for the holidays, just the weekends or perhaps a couple of months out of the year.

- **Choose your RV type** – Research each RV type and get familiar with what they have to offer and see what you are going to need for your everyday living.

- **Amenities check** – Before purchasing, ensure that your RV carries all the basic amenities that you have determined you need for the duration of your stay.

- **Budgeting** – Set a budget for the cost of traveling, groceries, repairs, and fixings and some for emergencies.

- **Choose your size** – Once you've decided on the type of RV you want, choose the size that is going to best fit your requirements.

- **Insurance coverage** – Scout around for the best insurance packages and prices and don't just settle for the first one that you see.

- **Market value** – If you are buying your RV, but you think that sometime in the future you could perhaps consider the possibility of selling it, research the models that offer the best resale value, so you don't lose a lot of money if you do decide to sell one day.

- **Inspection** – Have your RV thoroughly inspected and checked out by a trusted and reliable source before you confirm your purchase.

- **Test drive** – Before settling on a purchase, narrow down your RV choices to perhaps two or three options even if you know which one you already want. Take all three for a test drive to see if you happen to change your mind once you get the feel of the vehicle.

TEST DRIVE CHECKLIST

Once you've selected the models you want to take for a test drive, use this checklist for each model to ensure that these important aspects are all in working order:

- Start engine starts fine
- Headlights and fog lights in working order
- Door handles and locks function properly
- Automatic window controls all in working order
- Signal and brake lights are working
- Parking and backing lights are working
- Emergency lights are in order
- Air conditioner and heater works perfectly
- Window defroster works

- Parking brake release in working order
- Driver seat can be adjusted easily without struggling
- How the engine feels when on the move and the engine noise levels (if any)
- How quickly the braking and acceleration system responds
- How the steering wheel feels while in use
- Temperature gauges in working condition

BUYING A USED RV CHECKLIST

If you are buying a second-hand or used RV, keep an eye out for the following before making your purchase:

- Look for leaks or wall stains around the corners, windows, vents, and floors
- Check for dents, scratches, and stains and how severe they may be
- Ensure lights and fans are in working order
- Do the door hinges need replacing?
- Determine if the side mirrors allow good visibility
- Ensure the engine is able to start on the first try without any issues. Keep an ear out for any noises such as grinding, creaking, or clanging and other unusual noises that an engine is not supposed to make

- Test drive it up a hill and see how smoothly it still runs
- Determine that the brakes are still in top working condition
- Check if all the controls and windows are working
- Check if the steering wheel still works fine
- Check if the tires need replacing
- Check for any cracks that may be in the belts and hoses.
- Ensure that the exhaust emits clear and odorless smoke
- Is all the kitchen equipment like the refrigerator and oven still in working order?
- Check the water faucets, heater, and tanks for any leaks
- Determine that the water pressure is still good
- Check the holding tanks for leaks
- Check the condition of the floor and carpets (if any)
- Check the conditions of all the seats in the RV
- Determine that there is no rust on any of the exterior compartments
- Check that the sleeping spaces are in good condition
- Determine the condition of the vehicle and house batteries
- Ensure that the RV still has the original manuals for all appliances and equipment

And of course, never deal with an RV owner who is unreachable or that cannot be contacted easily if needed.

THE BASIC RV ESSENTIALS CHECKLIST

Your RV should come equipped with these basic necessities:

- First aid medication
- Folding chairs and tables
- Pots and pans
- Towels and blankets
- Brooms and dustpans
- Bug spray
- Cleaning supplies
- Electrical appliances
- Adaptors
- Extension cords and extra fuses
- Fresh water hose
- Matches and lighters
- Radio
- Sewer Hose
- Tire gauges
- Fire extinguisher
- Flashlight and batteries
- Paper plates and towels
- Pillows and bed sheets
- Trash can

- Trash bags
- Light bulbs
- Levelling blocks
- Basic toiletries kit
- Wheel chocks

The list would differ with each RV type and model. The more expensive models come with more amenities than, the simpler models, it would all come down to the type and size of the RV that you select.

PERSONAL SUPPLIES CHECKLIST

When you're on the road, there will be a list of things that you are going to want to bring with you while you're mobile. Remember that you may be halfway to your destination before you realize that you've left some important supplies behind and it could be too costly to turn around and get them. Having to buy new supplies would be an extra cost on your budget. Use this handy checklist guide to ensure you've got everything that you will need with you on hand:

- **Personal possessions** – This includes cash, checks, credit cards, keys, sunglasses, cell phone, cell phone charger, clothing and emergency clothing, camera and video equipment, medication and supplements, maps, guidebooks, and a compass.

- **Documentation** – Insurance proof, driver's ID, RV registration documents, tow vehicle contact numbers, road side assistance contact numbers, manuals to operate appliances and RV equipment, maps and travel guides.

- **Repair Tools & Equipment** – Sockets, duct tape, wrenches, hammer, screwdrivers, pliers, flashlight, batteries, pocket knife, clean rags, wheel wrench, jumper cables, motor oil, light bulbs, emergency flares, tire pressure gauge, coolant, jack, wire connectors, and cutters.

- **Sleep Comforts** – Extra pillows, bed sheets, blankets and bedspreads, alarm clocks and pajamas.

- **Kitchen Supplies** – Dishes, can opener, corkscrew, coffee, coffee pot, coffee maker, silverware, skewers, toaster, dish towels, containers and Tupperware's, napkins, cutting board, knives and tongs, zip lock bags, table cloth, picnic blanket and cleaning supplies

- **Other amenities** – BBQ set, tarp, extra tables and chairs, computer equipment, extension cords, bungee cords, pencils, paper, pens, and power adaptors.

- **Pet Supplies (if needed)** – Food stock to last the trip, food and water dish, litter box, doggy bags, leash, carrier, toys, collars, ID tags, and health certificates.

LEAVING HOME CHECKLIST

If you're not planning to sell off your home while you embark on your RV journey and have every intention of returning home one day, use this checklist before you hit the road to ensure that everything in your home is taken care of for your peace of mind while you travel:

- Turn off all the lights and fans
- Close all closets, drawers, and kitchen cabinets
- Lock each window securely
- Lock all the doors, including the garage door, securely
- Empty the trash from your home
- Clean up any mess before leaving
- Unplug all electronic equipment that you're leaving behind
- Turn off all the water faucets and main water line
- Set the alarm
- Give your neighbors your contact details and a number that they can reach you at for emergencies

CHAPTER FOUR

LEGAL CONSIDERATIONS & SAFETY GUIDES

LEGALITY CONSIDERATIONS OF RV LIVING

Before you hit the road, you are going to want to read up on the different laws and state statutes that you are going to encounter while living in an RV, especially if you are planning to do it full-time.

RV REGISTRATION AND INSURANCE

Insurance is of the utmost importance when you decide to hit the road in an RV. Just like a regular vehicle, RVs need to be insured against any potential accidents that could take place while you're driving or even sometimes while you are parked. Before you head out on your journey, ensure that your insurance documentation is up to date. You would also need to check the state laws where you are currently based and what the requirements may be for owning an RV to determine the type of insurance coverage you are going to need. If this is your first time owning an RV and you have some reservations about how to get started, so you don't run into any unforeseen issues, you could consider hiring the services of lawyers who specialize in RV accidents and injuries. They would be in a better position to offer legal advice and information that you may not have been aware of, especially when it comes to state-specific rights and insurance requirements. Buying an RV is just the first step of the process.

LEGAL CONSIDERATIONS OF LAND LEASING

Land leasing is an important legal consideration to consider. Because of the RV's size, naturally, it takes up a lot of space. Although the RV is your own, the land that you park your RV on is not. Which means it needs to be leased. It is important to pre-plan your trips so you will be able to make the necessary bookings and preparations beforehand to avoid any issues and complications that you would have to deal with upon arrival.

TENANT'S RIGHTS

Leasing the land to park your RV makes you a tenant. While some RV owners who have decided to go full-time with RV living prefer to buy the land that they plan to park on, if you are planning to constantly be on the move and on the road from one location to another, buying the land is not a practical option. As with renting any piece of property, you need to be aware of your rights as a tenant who is leasing a piece of land and ensure there is a clear-cut agreement drawn up between you and the landlord.

STATE LAWS

Each state would have their own set of laws, so to avoid a possible ticket, read up on each of the state laws before you head to them to ensure that every legal avenue is properly covered and taken into account. Among the things that could differ from state to state include warranties and road side assistance programs, as some states are more RV friendly than others.

RV SAFETY TIPS – A GUIDE TO DRIVING YOUR MOTORHOME SAFELY

Living on the road can be an amazing experience, but while you're having fun, don't forget to stay safe. A good RV trip is one that is well-thought out, planned and prepared for ahead of time so you can arrive safely with minimal problems faced along the way. Safety is paramount when you're on the road, especially if you have your family traveling with you.

TIP #1 – RV INSURANCE & ROAD SAFETY

Research the kinds of road side service assistance that are available, because not all road service companies would specialize in RVs. When picking out insurance, find an insurance company that is going to cover your RV and your trailer as well, covers vehicle towing or whether you would need a separate type of insurance to be eligible for road service coverage. Pick an insurance policy that is going to cover towing your RV, truck and the trailer as well to avoid the trailer that would be holding your possession in it from being left behind. Don't forget to check how far the road service assistance would be willing to tow your RV and trailer too.

TIP #2 – LEARNING TO DRIVE THE RV

You will soon quickly find that driving an RV is going to be very different from driving your average vehicle. It's going to require a whole new set of maneuvering skills because of the vast size some of these motor homes can come in. If this is your first time driving an RV, it is highly recommended that you do a few practice runs before you begin your journey. Consider renting an affordable RV for the day and drive around to get the feel for it. Start with a smaller RV for practice before you attempt any of the bigger models. As a first timer, you're going to quickly realize that it's going to require a lot of skills and concentration on your part to keep the lines while relying only on your mirrors to see what is happening behind you. Practice parking too, because parking your RV at a campsite is going to be different from cruising into a parking spot at the supermarket.

TIP #3 – PLANNING AHEAD

Make a list of the places you plan to go, check the locations you plan to park for the duration of your stay in that location and make reservations to book the place so your spot will be confirmed. Some campsites may not have a 24-hour check in, and the last thing you want is to find yourself stranded with no place to go. You also don't want to arrive at your designated campgrounds only to find there is no space for your RV because it's overbooked and you didn't call ahead to secure yourself a spot. Plan ahead and avoid any disappointments upon arrival.

TIP #4 – DON'T FORGET THE CHECKLISTS

Checklists are useful to avoid overlooking important details. You don't want to be miles on the road in the middle of nowhere before you realize there is a problem. Use a checklist before you leave your home, use a checklist to check your RV before you start your journey, and even bring a checklist with you on your journey as a helpful reminder of what needs to be checked and regularly inspected while on the move in your RV.

TIP #5 – CONSIDER RV TRAINING COURSES

Even driving a regular vehicle required driving courses before we could get our driver's license. And it is definitely worth considering taking up RV courses, especially if you are nervous about driving such a large vehicle for the first time. Some states in fact, require the driver to have an upgraded license to qualify driving an RV without any legal issues. Signing up an RV driving course may not be such a bad idea after all.

A BASIC GUIDE FOR RV SAFETY

Staying safe in your RV while on the road is easy, once you get the hang of it. Staying safe while on the road is a practice every RV driver should incorporate into their routine. If you find that all the rules and regulations are too overwhelming to take in all at one go, then just keep these 8 basic safety tips in mind to ensure every journey is your safest possible journey:

1. Before heading out, ensure the interior of your RV is secure, and everything is locked up as it should be, so nothing falls or moves around during the drive.
2. Always have extra supplies like batteries, food, and water on hand for every trip. If you find you are running low, stock up at your current destination before moving on to the next.

3. Map out your route ahead of time to avoid getting lost on the road or getting stuck in the middle of nowhere that could be miles from your intended destination.

4. Take adequate breaks and rest well the day before if you have a long drive ahead of you the next day. Never attempt to drive when you're feeling tired or drowsy especially when operating a large vehicle like an RV.

5. Keep a safe distance between vehicles in front of you because RVs take more time to slow down or accelerate in comparison to normal vehicles.

6. Maneuver corners slowly and carefully.

7. Know your RVs height to avoid crashing into low bridges.

8. Practice parking and braking as much as possible before you begin your journey. You'll be grateful that you did.

CHAPTER FIVE

PROS & CONS OF RV LIVING

J ust like everything else, living in an RV comes with its own set of ups and down, pros and cons. While living in an RV can be a wonderful adventure and an experience like no other, there are moments when it can be trying on the nerves, and it makes you wonder whether this was, in fact, such a good idea in the first place.

But first, let's start with the positives.

THE GOOD SIDE OF RV LIVING

The experience that you get traveling on the road in a mobile home is, of course, the most obvious pro. Experiences are priceless and something that no amount of money will ever be able to buy. You can either read about it in books or the internet, or you can go out there and live those experiences for yourself, and that is what RV living is all about. And while you're on the road, parked at different campsites or camp grounds, you have the opportunity to meet people you may not ordinarily have come across if you were just working your average 9 to 5 job. People from different walks of life, RV traveling for different reasons to discover their own purposes often have interesting stories and backgrounds to tell. And who knows, you could make a friend for life.

Another good perk that comes with traveling around in your mobile home is how much you would grow as a person after a couple of months on the road. The experiences that you pick up while on the road will leave you a different person from who you were when you first started your journey. Every experience that we encounter will inevitably leave an impact on us, whether good or bad. And there is no one who returns from RV life that can say they haven't changed as a person.

Living in an RV full time makes every day feel like a vacation! You are free to go anywhere you want, anytime you want, the world is yours for the taking. If you have ever dreamed of traveling across the country on the road, your RV will give you the chance to live out that dream. You get to bring the basic comforts of home with you AND bring your home (so to speak) with you everywhere that you go.

An RV is a smaller – much smaller – version of a home or apartment. A smaller space means quicker and faster clean ups. Instead of spending hours wearing yourself out scrubbing your home from top to bottom, it would take you less than 30 minutes to do a thorough cleaning of your RV, depending on the size of it of course. Score!

If you're traveling with a partner or your family, you find that you tend to communicate a lot more when you're on the road. For one thing, there's hardly any distractions around which means more attention can be focused on the people who are around you. There's no job, no stress, no television taking time away from your partner or family. The more you communicate, the closer you'll grow as a family. It's a great bonding experience. RV life also opens you up to communicating with new people, other RV travelers, as you share your stories and maybe pick up a few pointers. You will find that people tend to be a lot more open and eager to communicate when they are going through a similar experience. What's a better bonding session and conversation starter than life on the road as an RV traveler?

The thing about life on the road is, you start to really develop a sense of appreciation for the natural beauty you are surrounded by the more time you spend outdoors. Places outside the city have so much beauty to offer, and we get so caught up in everyday work routines, rushing from one place to another never stopping to fully appreciate what is around us. Living and traveling in an RV means you get out of the city a lot more and explore other parts of the country you wouldn't ordinarily do. Plus, being outdoors a lot with all that fresh air exposure (fresher than the city anyway!) leaves you feeling a lot healthier and much more relaxed as a person.

Experience is a great teacher, and there is no better way to learn new things than to experience them yourself. Having to go through the experience makes a lasting memory that you will never forget, and living life on the road as a traveler will teach you more in one year than an ordinary, everyday work routine ever will in several years.

THE DOWNSIDE OF RV LIVING

Now for the downside of RV living. For every pro, there is almost always a con, and RV living is no exception. True, the experiences and benefits that you stand to reap make it well worth it, but at the same time, it is good to have an idea of what downsides you may be in for when you decide to embark on this lifestyle.

The first and most obvious downside is being stuck in traffic. Being on the road a lot, it is a given that no matter how much you plan and prepare for a trip, there are going to be instances where you will end up stuck in jams that could last for hours.

Sometimes getting stuck in traffic is unavoidable. The cost of fuel is another thing you are going to have to be prepared for. Getting stuck in traffic costs a lot more fuel than you may have initially budgeted for during that trip. Before heading out on your journey, it is always good to budget with some extra funds for emergency situations like these.

Smaller spaces mean things and people will be getting in your way – a lot. Especially if you aren't traveling alone. Having a private or alone time is something you are going to have to wave goodbye to the minute you decide to live in an RV. Unless you're traveling alone of course. Even then, when you arrive at your destination, you won't technically be alone. Campgrounds would be filled with other people in their own RVs milling around. Be prepared to have peace and quiet be hard to come by. Smaller spaces also mean smaller shower and bathroom areas, and if you're used to having a full-sized bathroom like you normally do at home, this could prove to be quite an uncomfortable adjustment that is going to take some getting used to.

Sticking to your budget can be a tricky ordeal on the road, especially when unexpected expenses or repairs could crop up when you least expect it. Although this is easily resolved by budgeting extra for emergencies, it can still be a pain when you have to fork out some extra cash for situations that sometimes can't be avoided.

Driving around a big motorhome takes time to get accustomed to. Occasionally you may experience the frustration of finding it difficult to park or even to find an adequate place to park, and this is something you are going to have to be prepared to face frequently when you live in an RV. Driving an RV requires careful concentration and focus, and backing out of a parking space or even backing into one can prove to be a stressful ordeal just trying to make sure you don't hit anything as you do it.

Being on the move all the time also makes it hard for you to be contacted. Receiving mail, for example, decidedly becomes a lot harder when you have no fixed permanent address for delivery. Paying bills online becomes reliant on your ability to secure good internet connection, and even constant good internet connection like the kind you would get at home is something you are going to have to be prepared to let go off the minute you decide on a life on the road.

While at home, it may be easy for us to just head to the loo, do our business, flush and forget about what happens after that, living in an RV is something else altogether. Your sewage tank is literally going to be underneath you and it will be up to you to dispose of it accordingly when it gets near full or before it starts stinking up your RV. Having to handle your own waste can be a major turnoff for some people, because let's face it, it is a disgusting job. Just remember to hold your breath when you're emptying your sewage tank.

Despite all the cons, the pros of what you get from living in an RV far outweigh the cons, because if you really think about it, the cons are something that takes getting used to, and the great thing about people is, we always learn to adapt and adjust until we don't even notice it anymore.

CHAPTER SIX

BUDGETING, PLANNING & EXPENSES

Now it's time to talk dollars and cents. What exactly should you be planning and budgeting for when you live in an RV? This aspect is going to fluctuate depending on whether you are living in an RV full time or short term. Of course, long term RV living is going to require a bigger budget compared to if it was rented just for vacation purposes.

No one person's budget is going to be the same as another because everyone has their own sets of priorities and live different lifestyles from one another. Some people have more money to spend while others prefer to stick to a very specific budget and not deviate too much from it. Making and planning your budget and expenses is a very personal subject because you need to create one that is suitable for you.

One thing you are going to need to keep in mind about the RV lifestyle is, you are going to have to make some adjustments –

sometimes a lot of adjustments – to your current way of spending, especially if you are not going to have a steady job with a fixed paycheck coming in at the end of the month anymore. Although there are many ways for you to make a living while you are on the road and continue earning an income, it's still not a good idea to be carefree with your spending. Living in an RV is different from having a fixed routine, and unexpected situations and scenarios are a lot more likely to crop up while you're on the road.

Here's a look at what you can expect to spend when living in an RV and what to include as you begin to plan your budget, especially if you are planning on full-time RV living before you begin your RV journey:

THE BIGGEST EXPENSE

Your biggest expense is going to be your RV. If you have decided to purchase an RV to live in full time, this is going to be your biggest price tag, although it is no doubt much cheaper than owning a home. When executing this portion of your plan, you budget for not just the cost of the RV but the cost of the insurance and any other coverage you are going to need as well.

The first thing you should do is take a look at your current finances to see how much you can afford to spend on an RV. That would help you narrow down the type of RV that sits within your price range, and once you have decided on the model, it is easier for you to calculate the expenditure needed to secure the RV.

If you aren't paying cash in full, then look up the different bank loans, the monthly repayments involved and the interest that you would have to commit to and work that into your budget as well. Your budget when purchasing an RV should cover the following aspects:

- Price of the RV model
- Vehicle insurance
- Vehicle Registration
- Licenses you may need
- RV monthly fee repayments (if you've purchased your RV)
- RV monthly rental payments (if you're renting your RV for a short-term period)
- Security system (if any)
- Health insurance
- Extended warranty
- Towing insurance
- Mail forwarding service (because your mail has to go somewhere while you're on the road)
- RV Club dues

RV RUNNING EXPENSES

The expenses to run the RV that you would need to prepare for include the following:

- Gas/diesel
- Propane
- Campsite rental and overnight costs
- Upgrades
- Maintenance & repair
- Supplies & tools
- Road assistance membership
- Dump station fees
- Emergencies

DAILY RV LIVING EXPENSES

Expenses that you can expect to budget for while you experience life on the road include:

- Groceries
- Household items
- Internet
- Mobile phone bills
- Other food costs (fast food, take away and restaurant meals, etc.)
- Entertainment and recreation

- Clothing
- Laundry
- Toiletries
- Unexpected expenses
- Pets (if any)

Remember that budgeting is a very individual thing and no two budgets are going to be the same. The most important thing to remember is to always, always set aside a budget for emergencies and unexpected expenses. When you are on the road, often times there will not be an ATM machine or nearby bank that you can run to in the case of an emergency, so try to have some cash on hand with you at the start of each journey to avoid being caught in such a situation. An emergency fund is imperative because things could happen at any given time and it is always better to be over prepared than underprepared.

If after you have allocated everything you need to cover the major areas and still have some money left over for your savings, then congratulations! You're in the best position to start off your RV journey on a positive note. If you have drafted out a rough budget sheet and you find that your numbers are in the negative, you might want to take a moment to review if there are any other adjustments that can be made.

If you find that living in an RV full-time right from the get go may not be suitable for your budget at the current time, consider handling the process in stages and transition slowly into it until you can adjust your expenses accordingly. If you have considered living in an RV but have never done it before, try renting an RV and live in it for a couple of months to see if this is something that's right for you and something you want to fully invest in long-term. Always better to test the waters before fully jumping into something that is unfamiliar only to find down the road that it may not be suitable for you.

CHAPTER SEVEN

FOOD PREP & STORAGE TIPS

A s you probably already figured out by now, living in an RV isn't going to be the same as living in a home. A lot of adjustments needs to be made not just in your lifestyle, but in the way, you prepare and store food from now on too. Why? Because RV's come with kitchens that are much smaller than the average home, so small in fact that you may find a lot of the recipes you normally had no trouble preparing at home suddenly become a challenge or almost impossible to work with in an RV's kitchen.

The same goes when it comes to food storage. While a home comes with no shortage of kitchen cabinets and a large fridge for you to easily store leftovers, an RV kitchen does not. Space is scarce, so leftovers and food storage are going to be needed to be kept to a minimum because there simply isn't enough room to keep it all.

The best rule of thumb to keep in mind when planning for the kind of food you want to bring with you on the road is to keep it as simple as possible. The simpler, the better. Paper plates, cups, and plastic utensils are going to be your new best friends because they minimize the clean-up and save you water which is a precious commodity when you are living on the go and on the road.

FOOD STORAGE TIPS TO KEEP IN MIND

Tip #1 - An RV moves around a lot. Which means the food is going to get moved around a lot too, especially if it has not been properly stored away in cabinets or containers. Avoid keeping anything on the dining table or kitchen counters because if it isn't weighted down, you can bet that it is going to probably tip over and spill at some point. Food containers should be plastic, avoid glass at all costs because you run the risk of breaking them which is dangerous in a moving vehicle.

Tip #2 – Pack leftovers and edibles in baskets, cartons, Tupperware's, or zip lock bags. When on the move, store the containers away in the fridge or in the kitchen cabinets and make sure that they're secured in and won't budge even if the RV were to do one of those sudden brake stop maneuvers.

Tip #3 – Use lightweight tableware, tumblers, and containers whenever you can. Forget about heavy drinking glasses and large dishes, those need to be left at home because they simply are not practical for an RV.

Tip #4 – Avoid bringing raw meat and other high-risk perishables with you on the road. Not only does an RV fridge have limited space, but because you're on the move all the time, your fridge could easily get warm during the day, and that would risk ruining your food supplies. For RV living, it is best to opt for items that have a longer shelf life such as canned goods, crackers, cereal, oatmeal, instant cook meals, and even bread for example.

Tip #5 – Buying smaller packages may not be the most cost saving exercise, but in the attempt to save space in your RV, this is the best way to go. Pick smaller bottles and packets of the ingredients you may need for your meals and recipes, and only buy what you need.

HOW TO EAT HEALTHY WHILE LIVING LIFE ON THE ROAD

Sticking to a regular healthy meal routine while on the road can be something of a challenge. With all the gas stops and temptations for snacks at these stops, fast food, and selective food options because of a lack of space, the eating habits of RV travelers can easily be thrown off course.

Driving around in an RV means you're probably going to spend long periods of your time in sedentary positions, so it is important to try to stick to a healthy eating regime whenever possible to avoid health problems and weight gain down the road.

Tip #1 – If you feel the urge to snack, pick up a healthier snack instead. Snacks are great to have on hand while on the road because they can last for a long time without going bad and they don't require preparation. Luckily, there's no shortage of healthy snack options available. You could opt to:

- Make your own trail mix consisting of nuts, seeds, and dried foods. These are easy enough to throw together in a short amount of time. They taste good, and they're healthy too.

- Snack on more fruits and vegetables. Not only is it a great way to slip in your daily dose of vitamins, but fruits are high in nutrition, and they keep you feeling full.

- Pick protein bars that don't contain a lot of sugar in them. Read the ingredient labels at the back of the packs before you purchase them because you'll be shocked at how some protein bars can be up to 400 calories or more.

- Prepare sandwiches or wraps before the start of each trip. A simple tuna or chicken sandwich makes a great snack which can be stored for a longer period and doesn't require a lot of prep time or clean up afterward.

Tip #2 – Farmers markets are a great source for healthy food choices such as fruits, vegetables, and grains. They're modestly priced, and the ingredients are fresher with some places even offering organic options to choose from. It is also a great way to support the local state economy without doing too much damage to your food budget. Remember that you don't have a lot of space in your RV or fridge to store too much food, so buy only what you need to make it to your next destination.

MEAL PREP TIPS BEFORE HITTING THE ROAD

The best way to manage your meals while you're on the road is to plan and prepare each time you make a stop. Making a list of your menus and meal plans will give you a better idea of whether it is viable to cook and prepare it in an RV. Prepare a plan for your breakfast, lunch, and dinner with some snacks in between just in case you get the munchies before your next meal.

Keep the following tips in mind when meal prepping for your trip:

Tip #1 – Try sticking to one-dish meals. When meal prepping, one-dish meals are going to be the easiest and quickest option because you are cooking and preparing these meals in an RV. A quick search online will reveal dozens of quick and easy one-dish meal recipes for you to choose from.

Tip #2 – As you prep for your meals, cook an extra serving or two that can be stored as your next meal (but not too much, because remember space is limited). Check that you have enough containers and space in your fridge before you start cooking your meals and if you do, then go ahead and prepare an extra serving or two so you save yourself the trouble of cooking at every meal.

Tip #3 – The best way to meal prep successfully is to make a list of ingredients that you would need for the meals that you have in mind. Then take a look at the list again. If there is anything on that list that is easily perishable, cross it off the list and choose another recipe that is easier to prepare. Where possible, try to opt for meals that require more or less the same variety of ingredients. The more these recipes use the same ingredients, the fewer items you will have to keep in your RV. It makes things much easier food wise and storage wise.

Tip #4 – Keep the recipes you choose as simple as possible and a short list of ingredients.

Tip #5 – Pick a couple of menus and then rotate those menus while you are on the road. Not only will this avoid an unnecessary buildup of supplies that you need in your RV for cooking, but this ensures that you would use every item that you have purchased, so nothing goes to waste. And when you're living on a budget while traveling on the road, every cent you save goes a long way.

Tip #6 – A slow cooker is going to be one of your most useful tools during your RV life. If your RV has the space for it, then consider bringing it with you because it is a great alternative to using the stove. Plus, it gives you more options of food choices if you have this on hand with you. But only bring it with you if you have enough space to store it away properly.

CHAPTER EIGHT

EARNING MONEY ON THE ROAD

For a lot of travelers, getting to travel full-time without having to worry about income is a dream come true. True, it can be scary at first not getting a steady paycheck in every month, but luckily in this day and age, a steady paycheck from an office based job is not the only way one can earn a living.

BEFORE BEGINNING YOUR RV LIFE

Before you begin your life on the road, here are a couple of things you can do to bring in some extra cash to help you get started:

- **Sell Extra Stuff in Your Home** – Accumulated quite a bit of stuff you ended up not using that's just lying around the house. Sell it for some extra cash! Somebody else out there could be looking for something that you have for a fair price. Sell it online through Craigslist or eBay, hold garage sales in your front yard or ask your friends and family. At least you'll get some cash in hand, and the stuff doesn't go to waste.

- **Build a Steady Base of Freelance Work** – Freelance work is in abundance online, and it's a good idea to start building a steady client base a few months before you're planning to begin your RV journey. If you can get a couple of regular clients, who can provide a fair amount of work each month, great! Freelancing is a great way to make money from anywhere you are, and it's a great option for RV travelers because all you would need is a good laptop, a commitment to meeting deadlines and good internet connection.

- **Get Certified** – If you're able to, pick up some short courses or programs and get certified in additional skills that could be a useful contribution to potential workplaces. Getting certified gives you a leg up on the competition, and if you come with experience, you'd be a shoo-in for jobs that companies and employers need filling up.

- **Speak to Your Employer** – Before leaving your current job, if you have a good working relationship with your boss, have a chat with them to see if they would be open to the idea of you working remotely. Some companies may be more willing to accept the idea than you think, and it is worth a try. If your boss is open to it, you get the best of both worlds! A continued paycheck monthly while living your dream of being on the road in your RV.

WORKING WHILE ON THE ROAD

- **Seasonal Work** – If you get lucky, you'll be able to score the occasional seasonal jobs that some RV campgrounds and campsites may have available during your stay.

- **Teaching Online** – Do you have a special skill set? Or an area of expertise that is your specialty? Online courses are growing in popularity, and the great thing about it is, you can teach a course from anywhere you are as long as you have a good internet hookup. Once you've built up a steady following or enough experience, you can even create your own online courses for some extra cash.

- **Temp Jobs** – As you travel from state to state, if you're considering staying on for a couple of weeks or more, consider picking up some local temp jobs for some extra cash. It won't be any fancy, high flying positions, but hey, at least it's some extra cash in your pocket at the end of the day, and depending on the job, you could gain some interesting new experiences and skills to talk about at your next family gathering. Sizeable cities are your best bet for a constant demand for temp workers to fill up certain positions for a short amount of time. Check with the local temp agencies of the states you're stopping in to see if there's anything that could be right up your alley.

- **Shift Work** – If you don't mind the odd hours, retail outlets and restaurants are a good option for part-time work you can pick up along the way as you travel.

- **Freelance Jobs** – If you've already started on this even before you gave up your full-time job, find more freelance work and clients who can provide consistent work, so you always have a means of earning some money. The more clients you pick up, the more money goes into your pocket.

- **Telecommuting Jobs** – Craigslist has plenty of telecommuting jobs just waiting for the right candidates to take up. Just like freelance work, finding and building a good relationship with the people you work with is the key to keeping your clients coming back to you or even retaining you for a long-term period.

- **Become a Virtual Assistant** – Virtual assistant jobs are growing in demand, and if you've got exceptional organizational skills with a talent for multitasking, getting a job as a virtual assistant could be the right fit for you.

- **Sell Images Online** – If you've got a good camera and a talent for taking just the right images captured at the right moment, there are several online websites that you could sell this images to. The great thing about being on the road and living in an RV is that you'll have no shortage of images to capture and the earning potential here could be very promising indeed.

- **Blogging** – Share your adventure with other readers who may be thinking about taking up the RV life by blogging about your experiences while you're on the road. Although blogging could take a while before you see a steady flow of cash coming it, it is a great way to get started on an additional passive income.

Making a living while living on the road is not impossible, as long as you have the perseverance to keep going. Because you're constantly on the move and not relying on a stable job, you need to remember not to rely on just a single income source. Take on as many jobs as you can, especially if you're freelancing and try to create a diversified source of income, so there is always money coming in from somewhere.

To make a living while you travel around in your RV would also require you to keep an open mind and be willing to try new things. Remember that there will be times you're going to have to take on jobs you may not necessarily like and it could take a while to get used to this kind of lifestyle. You would also need to be a lot more proactive and a lot less picky, otherwise you're going to have a tough time trying to secure constant work to keep up with your RV life.

CONCLUSION

Thank you again for choosing and making it through to the end of this book, let's hope it was informative and able to provide you with all the tools you need to achieve your goals whatever they may be. Whether you are looking to purchase your first RV, trying to decide if the pros of RV living outweigh the cons, or even if you just need a checklist to refer to, remember to bring this book along with you on your travels, so you always have a handy guide by your side anytime you need it.

The next step is to start sorting out what your needs and requirements are going to be for life on the road and research the best RV model that is going to be able to meet your needs. The tips and suggestions provided in this book were designed to serve as a guideline and a reference of the most basic and important information you are going to need for you to refer to so you have a better idea of how to get started. There's a lot of information, advice, and suggestions about RVs and what it is like living in an RV full time, and it can be tricky to determine which points would be of best use to you. I hope this book has helped.

Made in the USA
Middletown, DE
08 September 2017